In the Vision of Birds

new and selected poems

By the Same Author

POETRY

Late Romantics (with Robert Allen and Mark Teicher)
the hills that pass by
Iridium
Luna Moth and Other Poems

ANTHOLOGIES

Saturday Night at the Forum
Full Moon: an anthology of Canadian women poets
(edited with Janice LaDuke)

Acknowledgements

Many of the poems in this collection, or earlier versions of them, appeared in the following books: *Late Romantics* (with Robert Allen and Mark Teicher), 1981; *the hills that pass by,* 1987; *Iridium,* 1993; and *Luna Moth and Other Poems,* 2004.

Many also appeared in *The Fiddlehead, Jacket* (Australia), *The Louisville Review, Matrix, The Moosehead Review, Poetry Quebec, Sidestreet,* etc.

Philip Lanthier was founding editor of the literary magazine *Matrix* and has written and lectured on Eastern Townships poetry. He has a doctorate in English from the University of Toronto, has taught at Champlain College and Bishop's University, and now runs the annual literary event, Knowlton WordFest.

STEVE LUXTON

In the Vision of Birds
new and selected poems

WITH AN INTRODUCTION BY PHILIP LANTHIER

LIVRES DC BOOKS

Cover art by Carol-Anne Pedneault.
Author photograph by Angela Leuck.
Book designed and typeset by Primeau Barey, Montreal.
Edited by Angela Leuck.

Legal Deposit, Bibliothèque et Archives nationales du Québec
and the National Library of Canada, 2nd trimester, 2012.

Library and Archives Canada Cataloguing in Publication
Luxton, Steve, 1946-
In the vision of birds: new and selected poems / Steve Luxton.
ISBN 978-1-897190-84-5 (bound).
ISBN 978-1-897190-83-8 (pbk.)
I. Title.
PS8573.U9815 2012 C811'.54 C2012-902332-9

For our publishing activities, DC Books gratefully acknowledges the financial support of the Canada Council for the Arts, of SODEC, and of the Government of Canada through the Book Publishing Industry Development Program (BPIDP).

Canada Council for the Arts | Conseil des Arts du Canada

Société de développement des entreprises culturelles Québec

Printed and bound in Canada by Groupe Transcontinental.
Interior pages printed on FSC® certified environmentally responsible paper.
Distributed by LitDistCo.

FSC www.fsc.org MIX Paper from responsible sources FSC® C011825

DC Books
PO Box 666, Station Saint-Laurent
Montreal, Quebec H4L 4V9
www.dcbooks.ca

In memory of Robert Allen,
1946-2006.

Thanks for help, advice,
and inspiration to Robert Allen,
and also to Keith Henderson,
Angela Leuck, Jan Draper,
Philippe Barey, Diane Primeau,
Bill Furey, and so many others.

Contents

VII. What the Landscape Wants

Introduction–Bush Lyrics

Poetry comes to Steve Luxton with a sudden surprise. It "visits" when he's tramping through fields and woods; it "arrives" in a "scented spring dawn" as he moves through tall grass towards the chanting of hundreds of peepers. When they abruptly stop, everything goes silent, and there is a moment of "perfect intimacy with strangeness." This is of the essence of his work: nature "gathers him in"; gives him "poise." There are no gods anymore, he says, just such moments when we stand transfixed by "this world of fine, pure solitude." With this collection of poems, nearly all of which have an eye and an ear on the natural world, his stature as of one of Canada's most observant and entertaining voices is confirmed.

One of his favorite poems, "Citycountry" describes a climb up a stream bed behind his cabin after a storm. He's a "green apostle," a "wide-eyed eremite" [hermit] chanting to himself in the post-storm twilight. Then panic sets in. He's been here before and recalls the "bush lyrics" he voiced "in a velcro and video age" but thinks it's all "swamp loco" and "plain loopy." An image of the city rises fantastically above the bushline to poison the twilight. In the city he's a firefly on a downtown corner; in the country he's a street lamp over a beaver pond. "I'm an outlander in two different / sites of dreams," he writes, though at the top of the trail, his mind comes to rest and appears to accept the fusion of the two equally fantastical dream sites. Hiking up the hill turns into a "hike through a skyscraper's heart." The fused words in the title signal the collapsed distinctions inherent in the poet's inescapable "outlandish" condition.

This, perhaps, is the plight of the modern pastoral poet. The world continues to be too much with us, and any attempts to dedicate ourselves–"green apostles"–to the elemental gods of rock, field and stream may induce states of self-mockery rather than devotion. The poem's witty word choice–vamp, loopy, loco, busted–tells us that the voice of the poem is not only that of an outlander, but somewhat outlandish as well.

The dialectic between town and country, society and solitude, streetlights and fireflies goes back a long way and has been an extraordinarily fertile source of poetic inspiration. Pastoral poetry originated with the third century BC Latin poet Theocritus whose bucolic idylls celebrated the lives of shepherds within an idealized and tranquil natural setting well removed from the troublesome world of city and court. Since then, pastoral poetry had has a long and various history in many languages. In English, such poetry flourished in the work of Spencer and Milton, later with Wordsworth and Shelley, and later still with Robert Frost, Gary Synder and Seamus Heany. Over the centuries it has come to be applied to any work in which the speaker of the poem has withdrawn from the meretricious, complex and conflicted world to a place closer to the elemental rhythms of nature. Doing so, the poet may be rewarded with a heightened sense of self and a clearer insight into existence. Or perhaps not, nature being of uncertain behaviour and the poet incapable of sloughing off the burdens of city life. The Latin term *otium* has been assigned to the state of mind which ensues from such a withdrawal. It can mean vacant time, simple leisure, retirement, or a state of contentment and mental self-sufficiency. In English poetry, the most striking example of *otium* may be found in Andrew Marvell's poem "The Garden" in which the speaker finds himself stumbling over melons, enjoying the fall of apples on his head and the arrival of peaches and nectarines which have happily reached into his hands. In such a pleasurable and passive condition, the mind annihilates "all that's made / To a green thought in a green shade."

The Eastern Townships of Quebec have been home to the green thoughts of a number of distinguished Canadian poets writing in English, notably John Glassco (1909-1981), Ralph Gustafson (1909-1995) and D. G. Jones (1929-). There is something about the Townships which has nourished such poets and each in his distinctive way has imaged its gentle northern Appalachian terrain in verse. Jones has addressed the changing nature of pastoral in his poem "A Garland of Milne" which reformulates Margaret Atwood's satiric take on the pioneer attitude towards the land. In "Progressive Insanities of a Pioneer" she imagines a geometrically fixated male persona who would impose lines and fences on the "totally en- / closed" spaces in the middle of nowhere. As his "green vision" disintegrates, he goes mad, bushed by the refusal of the land to bow to his wishes. The poem is an instructive gloss on the Townships, which were originally laid out in tidy 100 square mile cantons by surveyors, then re-divided into twenty-eight lots of 100 acres, the rest being assigned to the church or left "wild." Jones's counter poem to Atwood's essentially feminist view imagines the land as transformed visually by Canadian artist David Milne: "He lived in the bush, the wilderness / but he made light of it.... He let the trees stand where they were." His Milne persona goes quietly and lies in wait for "the still / moments when the snow / fell from the branches."

Steve Luxton advances the Arcadian experience deeper into the wild, at least what wild still remains available in the Eastern Townships, and where he can find it in its more dramatic form farther afield in Canada and the United States. He invites the reader to share in a paradoxical and metaphoric walk into the forests, up stream beds, across fields skirted by bushlines in all kinds of weather. Yet this is not a one-way amble. We are not merely moving carefully and observantly through the terrain; nature is, in a profound sense, walking through us as well. The terrain is experienced on the ground in moments of intense awareness. Like Jones's Milne he goes still, moves slowly, watches and listens. He opens himself to the intimations of the ripples, shivers, vibrations and inhalations of the animal and vegetable world. On the other side, Nature is a living presence, insistent and watchful, poised and Other, though not completely so. We are part of it; it is part of us. If the term ecopoetry applies to his work, then Luxton is an organism within our regional biosphere experiencing "a sheer wild intercession," a form of secular prayer uniting us with our fellow organisms. He connects to the land viscerally. He knows it loves us, but if we don't love it back, if we leave it in the dust as we retreat down the road in our technological bubble, the loss will be catastrophic. "It lunges / after us longingly / like a dog after / a familiar pick-up truck." Poor dog. Stupid truck.

Luxton is well aware of the dangers of easy sentimentality or the pose of detachment which renders the world merely picturesque. In "Postlude" he accuses Wordsworth of spending more time "inditing about glades than rambling in them," then adds "Me too!" admitting that the poet's job is getting Nature down on the page. What Luxton does is to convince us that he's been there, that we are in the presence of a voice coming from ground or stream level which has learned the country not by rote, but by heart. Like the rest of us, the persona is a bit of a klutz at times, stumbling into ravines, slipping on rocks, making discoveries which might otherwise not have occurred. Nevertheless, you are comfortable with him as you would be with an outdoorsman who knows his way around and has invited you for a walk in the woods.

But along the way what crazy talk, what happy lingo! When Luxton enters a shamanistic mode he can become both rhapsodic and goofy, loco in a sky-high poetic sense. The language is concrete, physical, and witty. It tells us things about animals and birds and what it's like to hear coyotes croon, glimpse the "redundant craze" of a moose's antlers and how spiders, like sailors, "know the ropes," how for a mink, life is "wriggle and squeeze" in its crawl space, how the brook trout rise in moonlight "like monks at a midnight communion," and how the Abenaki gods may still lurk in curling water fog. His figures of speech delight with their surprising and unexpected linkages: the "dolorous face of a bull moose"; an owl making a sound like a departmental photocopier; a salmon "muscling toward a fathering extinction"; cirrus clouds so high they appear to be "sky-silk / combed off another planet." Luxton's voice moves with great aplomb through a range of styles: demotic, reflective, self-deprecating, and hallucinatory. When he allows his language to take a deep breath and exhale in a shamanistic transport, the results are wild, comedic and exhilarating.

Take a look at another acknowledged favorite of his, "Loony Tune." This is a poem which Luxton reads aloud with considerable brio (give it try and see what happens) and which takes the form of a rambunctious performance celebrating the springtime moon. That moon becomes "Big Momma Lou… queen of the ball… the big D.J. in the sky" and we all join in a communal "boogie" in a Dionysiac Saturday night at the bandstand with Stravinsky and Sylvester the Cat. Luxton's sound effects are fun, his references to pop culture animate up the verse, give it a surprising zap. Wordsworth, who preferred to evoke Nature in tranquility as a consoling and revelatory memory, is a mere wallflower here. "Mildewed old hypocrite" is what he calls him in "Postlude," though he may simply be in a quarrelsome mood.

In Canada we are familiar with the term "bushed" as it applies to being driven crazy by the solitude of the wilderness. It has provided the title of at least three poems by Canadians, most notably Earle Birney's 1952 version featuring a mountain so big and alive that it spooks the protagonist, slows his mind down when he looks at it, and sends out booming "proclamations at noon." It then shapes its peak into an arrowhead to "come singing into his heart." Not completely mad, this bushed man is something of a proto-poet who unconsciously possesses the kind of sensibility which Wordsworth imagined in another key: "I heard among the solitary hills / Low breathings coming after me, and sounds / Of undistinguishable motion." Wordsworth's landscape is moralized. The huge peaks are after him because he's taken a boat when he shouldn't have. Birney's figure is psychically overwhelmed by the sheer immensity of everything.

Steve Luxton's nature poetry is "bushed" in a sense not too far removed from Birney. Not addled by isolation or driven bananas by the incursions of nature on his carefully nurtured square of land, he goes into the bush to find out what's what and to put the best words to it. Yes, it drives him slightly loco, but the language transfigures the madness and makes it a song of praise and acceptance. At the same time, he knows what's happening in the countryside that's still left open to us. There are poems which tell of the depredations of ATVs, the dangers of getting shot, run over, or beaten up by bikers guarding their pot fields. Read his ingenious curse delivered to the man who despoiled a favorite stream with an autoroute overpass.

There is, of course, a personal dimension in his poetry. As you read through this collection, you will note the progression from animals to neighbours to friends and lovers. There are poems marking his fortieth and sixtieth birthdays, poems lamenting the departure of lovers and a heartbreaking poem recalling poet Rob Allen (1946-2006). Leaving the dying man, "grey and fleshless," Luxton seeks consolation in country chores, but his truck goes off a logging road into a ditch. He reaches for his cell phone to call his "oldest, dearest buddy" then realizes that they will "never / race across far hills / to rescue each other again." This is a sharply felt moment of loss with none of the consolations available through the conventions of an extended elegy, simply the pang of total absence triggered by, of all things, a cell phone.

These are poems which take time to reflect on the life of poetry and the realization of loss and mortality. In "Crouching Tiger (Written on turning 60)" he asks himself what he is seeking in the "glimmering / thinning realm" of the fall foliage, somewhat Chinese in its superb crimsons and gold: fame? riches? restorative waters? or a fat Buddha in a clearing who may reveal the mystery? There is no answer, simply the discovery of a heron's nest and an abandoned backpack, perhaps all that we should expect or deserve. In "This Life," as he walks across a moonlit riverbank littered with May ice, he wonders whether everything is "luminously meaningless, protean / evanescent, sited in a Cosmos / like some endlessly unfolding, exploding diagram." It is strange, it is odd. The intimations of a dark vacancy in the universe may be "appalling." There is, again, no answer except the "swish" of blood waltzing in his head amid the immense silence. Beauty helps, so does a little companionship.

In the final piece of this selection, a prose poem entitled "Milby Swamp" which describes one of his typical walks, he's in search of late winter comfort but fears that "Everything slips away relentlessly." Lovers, mentors are gone; his youthful sense of the sweetness and newness of nature has been "stymied." But then he senses the flowing water at his feet, the return of creatures thought long gone, the way that wild things "huddle, drowse and dream," and he finds that he has never left, that the beaver hutch he has to his surprise discovered is where he has lived all this time "beside the surging stream." The poem makes a strong and affirmative finale to his ruminative woodland explorations. Even as time does its inevitable damage, he can still be startled by new discoveries.

Notes of the pastoral tradition still echo in these poems, even those of that old hypocrite William Wordsworth, not to mention poets like Al Purdy, Earle Birney, Don McKay, D. G. Jones, Gary Snyder and Ted Hughes. But Luxton has brought his own distinctive music and voice to the Arcadian theme. These poems are deft, fresh, inventive, funny, sad, and fully informed by the lore learned in the woods, fields and streams. Read them silently or aloud. Remember them when next you go for a walk on a mountain trail or follow a curling stream at dawn.

Philip Lanthier, Brome Lake, Quebec, April 2012

I. Mink Song

In My Fever

(After a Cree Poem)

In my fever
was born a man
from the belly of a trout.
He entered a riffle.
He was invisible
like gold dust.
He did not know my face.
It was me I saw.

Dreaming another time
I saw a man born
in a ground-hog hole.
He woke alone.
He shivered at the sight
of the wind.
The motion through grass
was of badgers,
weasels.
In my fever
it was me
they headed for....

In my fever
I dream these things.

Recurrent

Again he dreams of a big, bedraggled bear
rearing puzzled in a clear-cut,
bellowing and pawing the air,

still roaming
along ridgelines, down sags, through pine barrens,
in search

of the honey hoard he feels
sure is hid somewhere
in the old Dead Tree Trunk of the World.

Silver Whiskers

The purpose of animal whiskers
is to gauge crawl-space widths.

Sepulchered a year
in a cedar trunk hole,
this mink
waxes pharaonic.

Gone the feline sinews,
the lithe flesh
fattened on mice and trout,
then spring-water slaked,
moulted the furrier's plume,
once svelte ermine.

Rigid on my palm,
mighty Cheops in miniature,
time-stiffened,
grave robbed,
plundered,
except for marvelous,
intact, silver whiskers.

Re-interring you in your niche,
late-potentate,
I get the message
of your immortal crypt:
strait is the gate.

You were despot of this swamp,
yet life was still
wriggle and squeeze
through low portals
and long tunnels with little width.

Beaver

Making snow angels
I envision them below
in their deep bulbed solitudes

–monks
at work by the light
of the will-o'-the-wisp,

with spring-steel nibs
on birchbark
rendering fabulous wild touches

to The *Parliament of Beastes*
or some splendid *Wilderness Regained,*

a gorgeously illustrated classic
wherein all traps
lie broken

while the fiends plunge
from their heights at last
howling through human faces.

Night Score

Over the dim lake
an owl muses complacently.

Too-wit, too-woo
–what a grand world this is
with its satin-skinned mice
to pluck off the rocks.

Behind the hill
three coyotes
croon of marrow
and red deer wreckage.

Beyond my campfire
a hungry pike plucks.

Tossing fish bones to the flames
I hum what I know:
The beauty of this world is matchless
–a lullaby of throes.

To See a Bull Moose

Forget it!
Walk low, wet country, distracted
by, say, the wig of foam twirling on a riffle,
rough swathe in the grass left
by a slouching snapping turtle.

Come to the farthest
reach of your planned walk
then fretfully turn, in your head too,
back to the usual concerns:
unanswered e-mails, fatty diet, taxes, death.

Soon, it is like someone upstream
blew the big old beaver dam,
floating the sky-high
pile in the barn
through the kitchen into the bedroom!

Worry even more, stop noticing anything,
talk to yourself out loud, at odds,
certainly not watching your step,
so that raving away on a ravine slope,
you trip, roll cursing down

onto a river shoal, where once,
crisp with hope, you trout fished but got bug bit,
lie stunned among fever orange jewel-weed,
oddly shaped spikes of driftwood,
a sucker corpse gone putrid.

Suddenly a bull moose,
not thirty paces off, eight feet tall,
head burdened by a redundant
craze of antlers swung your way,
now long-legging it slowly east,

face dolorous, curious, like the long-nosed
kindly deacon who once discovered you,
bright kid with a sure thing future, fallen
spread-eagled at the foot of the school steps,
bloody-kneed, dazed, unsure of where he was.

Spider Bend

Where the Tomifobia hooks,
a rock maple tilts,
webs rigged over every crotch.

Rising daylight reveals
a full-sailed galleon!

From upriver, a dawn wind
gusts through the narrows,
rakes the bank ferns,

showers up night-dew,
clouds of drugged,
slowly spinning flies....

Spiders, like sailors, know the ropes.
White webs fill, gorge with bugs,
hungrily, like huge cheeks.

Mink Song

To my preys' vast relief,
snow caves under my feet
and vanishes me.

Still, they'll come to grief.
I'm now
inside the drift,
unerring ears pricked

for the patter of tender mice feet,
exultant thump of rabbits
relieved they're
delivered from me.

My fearsome top-side stealth
froze their blood,
now watch *this*–

subnivean, subzero terror,
explosive upward seizure.
Ahhh! Bloody bliss.

Now, swallowed deep in winter,
I drift satiated up
star-pale tunnels and dream
of disemboweling the moon.

Boreal Phantasmagoria

On the river trail past dark
a phosphor moon
in fresh snow-piled
deadfalls… runes!

I am deciphering
difficult silver texts
when, brushed with frost,
a fox leaps forth,

folkloric phantom,
snow ploughs down a drift,
looks back once, skidding,
darts upstream on the
first edge of winter ice.

Seized, unable to divine
that jagged red gaze,
I halt on the trail,
when, with a tinkle-crash,
edged like fantastic green-blue glass,

a piece of ice (split off),
comes floating dead-silent by,
fresh Antarctic raft,
the fox ice-borne,
legs splayed,

pointy snout thrust down,
eyes glancing up from under
with another inscrutable intensity,
all the way down
to the next fast bend of the river.

II. Old Fisherman

Old Fisherman

In that country of sunken rivers
he awoke one morning
to the full sound of a stream.

Nowhere close by
could he recall abundant water.

But there, in the scarred
geography of his hand,
something brightened
like an old desire
or a re-opened wound.

Down the eskers of his fingers, his thumb,
brooks descended palmward
into a perfect silver pool.

Something else flashed.
Circling, a great trout,
terribly small.

Gothic Piscatorial

The stars emerge
over the private brook.
Big bow-backed trout
slip from the shadow of stones
to gather in the lit pool.
They spread like a black lacquer fan
across dim currents
that tickle and ease them
like the hand of a lordly angler
stirred by hungry dreams.
Here in a beleaguered band,
they pass the night
feeding fussily
but with vicissitude's sharp appetite,
and brooding behind scarred lips
upon a lifetime of caution:
the ferocious self-discipline
which brilliantly preserves
their straitened, gallant portion.
Few beings know such lonesomeness,
yet in this blue pool
a pure camaraderie coheres
among those who've endured
on the estate of some predatory knight
now sleeping off his trout-flesh with one care....
Gorgeous generations darted here
until the final deadly jerk.
In the brief interval, in subsided fear,

they rise to pale starlight
settling like a ghost mayfly hatch.
Like monks at a midnight communion
they feast on silvery nothings here.

The Angler Reconnects

Blinded again by water-beauty,
I forget, like love,
trout fishing demands
deft approach and presentation.

Semi-tufted nub, my head's silhouette
broaches the pool.
My rod's whip follows, slicing
across the stream's swift lights.

Still stalking,
eyes out for slick stones,
feet hopping mauve-brown holes,
I spot the flitting of a telltale shadow!

Fish darting below,
or bird crossing above?
Eyes heavenwards, I go down full length,
just in time grab my flyaway glasses.

Now the trout are out of their holes!
Hauling myself out, dripping,
confirmed klutz, I crouch
on a big bird-whitened boulder,

thinking maybe this is no longer
a profitable expenditure of my time,
when suddenly I miss my wallet.
No, it's here still, dry but empty.

Then I spot my money, my identity card,
plus all its lurid plastic kin, flocking
to that wonderful multi-coloured shindig
in the sunlit whirlpool downstream.

The Fisherman

What do I look for
in these rivers and chill ravines,
scuffing through tracts of sparse trilliums?

I delve here, dip in there
like a perfect disbeliever.
Ignoring "No Trespass" signs
I hurry into waders.

Brimming with blue and green
I doze in far motels
with a map over my face.

Who has whose number–I,
or some trout
with a jaw to crush the yearning?

What am I looking for
down these rivers and damp ravines?
Somewhere my maps can't show?
An estate I've not yet entered,
not yet been: a bridge
of thick water
across sunken dreams?

At the River's Side

This spring, I'm back.
Alone.

There are the willows'
felted blooms,
unraveling green cresses,
and a cold-slugged trout.

He's one of those who,
last fall,
swaggered brilliantly around our thighs,
still unhooked.

Reawakened to life's
next passion and amnesia,
he remains a sojourner in the river
of all things hurrying past
except for a startling moment, him,
alone once more
at the first and last.

Three Canoeists after Dinner

The tents up, the trout eaten,
we stand where gnarled granite
slides through the white shadow of the moon
into the lake.

Satiated now
one of us stares one way,
his neighbour another.
Stoned, we pose slightly askew
where owls and loons soothsay
along twisting lanes of water.

I've just looked up.
I'd spotted minnows below,
sipping the reflections of the stars
while among them a jackfish
made dark and thrusting slaughter.

At the Office

I camp at my desk, paper-dammed, and sigh.
Beyond the ceiling grate, the unseen fan churns
like a river escaping
an impounded, silted watershed.

Here, among leaning book stacks,
an unread two-sheet update
on my forever impending pension,
I do fuck all,
fritter away time folding
an origami canoe light and slim
enough to portage past the vent.

Fall: Voyaging into the Wind

I tie in the pack and push off with care.
Still, the canoe keel scrapes sand like
the brush of my dead father's cheek.

Against the gunwale my paddle's helve grieves.
As I quarter the big lake, swerving winds
raise white-hackled, tricky
cross waves....

To reach the sheltering headland,
I dig long and deep,
groan like a heavy-laden hinge.
Just outside the point's lee, something banks,
clattering in,

grabs my trouser shank and
hangs on for dear life
to rest a moment.

–Egg-brittle blue, body all pinched waist,
a dragonfly,
wings half tatters,
but still outstretched and glistening.

III. Near Neighbours

Ode to a Country Stone Pile

Here is an altar of the world's bones.
This red sun-up along the scrubby
pasture's edge,
it mounds and elbow-curves
at length and with grace,
like a giant's cast-off limb
or the shape of the limit of throwing
by dead-tired men on tractors and carts
at long furrow's end.

From fractured glacial-scatter
they have fashioned the white arm
of the Great Being
–like paleontologists
who rebuild thunder-lizards
(remodelled obscurely on themselves...)
from a single chalky femur.

Six layers of simple Sawyerville farmers
had other things on their minds
as they cast about!
Intent on their plough's stony road
they sculpted their worship mound
sidelong and perfectly unknowing.

Dying Farmer

To Lawrence Draper

Ruder than first growth
his brushy pasture
cavorts before him,
tree-dreaming and waiting.

His days are field stones
stacked in each fence corner
(high as a man's bones)
but tumbled now
and a-scatter.

He sobs and kicks.
Out of its niche
a snake comes dancing

down the wreck
that pinned the farmer's will
among the rebound
of hungry hills.

Cold Spell

The pump on Arty Walker's land has split,
he claims, though locals purse their mouths at it.
For what I'm worth–the new guy–it's so cold
that, Sunday, stuck to shed roofs where they'd lit,
I counted maybe three score freeze-dried tits.

Old Arty's just a shirker: it ain't the cold,
men say. If every lame excuse he's told
of busting frost and parching drought were true,
he wouldn't have to pull up stakes and fold.
He'd be mining tall tales out there like gold.

Maybe. Aged syrup's drunk here. Mine's brand new.
Arty *is* strange. His bit of hill and slough's
no sparser than my own. In lonesome fact
they are my own. We share and bear a view
of seeps and sags and ridges heaped up blue.

But the folks like things simple here, a lack
if more than cars or beer eases your back.
Claims my eccentric friend: They're so damn tight
they stuff their imaginations in a sack
and snuff them with the cat's new brood out back.

Now that's daily lingo from one too bright
to drown his mythic oddness; who thought he might
warm through fancy this cold section alone.
Hell, he intones, the winter here's no fight
compared to the bushels dumped on your light.

Fancy alone.... Huh! Shaking my head home
drunk but not enough, I start a flat-out croon
mimicking the wind in the stuck blue trees,
trying through forlorn heightening to loan
this severe spot an art enough for me.

Spring Resurrection

The budding woods shine.
Fall seems forgotten,
even forgiven.

Along the woods trail,
two foraging rabbits
still silver-splotched

calmly side-glance me by.
Browsing the brush edge, a big buck
(as if recalling some atrocity)

stiffens a grim moment
then eases,
sensing no peril.

–By Time's grace,
on fresh sufferance,
it seems I've regained

admission to Nature's
glistening refurbished feast.
I savour each vouchsafed step,

when, suddenly over the ridge: POP, POP, POP!
Taking his first May spin,
some local on his ATV

tire-flattens empty beer cans
scattered, no doubt, along with shell casings
by last fall's hunters.

The rabbits flee.
Again the buck freezes,
swings towards the big nearby swamp

–refuge of beings persuaded
humankind is of the same stamp....
Shrugging and spreading my palms wide, I

make a dumbshow of innocence.
He suddenly stops short,
peers momentarily over his silver scut

–from reflex, likely–
then whomps off
leaving me empty-handed.

So I crook my arms
and mime
a well-aimed, lethal shot.

Near Neighbours

Deep in the pasture at night,
hands grasping hips, I rotate,
peer up through a bald-topped pine,
whirl the stars, or squat
and loudly chant: "Om."

I exercise and meditate back here because,
one night, driving home,
the newly widowed farmer up the hill
spotted something weird along the river road
–a sort of eastern Sasquatch or bush-demon–
performing odd rites.
He nearly lost the road as it dived from his brights.

But he was alright.
Ducked in the muddy ditch, me too.
I guess, home safe, he must have figured
what he'd really seen,
though he never *directly* raised it with me.

–Several times, however, up
in his increasingly messy kitchen,
after he'd pulled out a dozen beer,
and told me now Alice was gone
the dog was acting *off*
–maybe slipping away and
running deer with coyotes at night,

and allowed how it was rough going
caring now for the cattle and farmhouse both
(where the hell *was* that bottle popper?),

he'd mention tales he'd heard
of aging hippies and "tree-huggers" who'd
moved into the Townships years ago
and how strange some had got,
living too long by themselves and
smoking all that funny tobacco.

Pastoral

Seeking advice on a good walk,
I drop in next door where
Old Ted in the back room slumps before his TV.

Stay off that new "Green"
hike and bike only trail, he says.
Local punks don't like it.
They'll run their ATVs
right over top of you!

What about the fields?

Nope, keep clear of *them*
–especially in corn.
It hides Bikers' pot.
Doped-up, crazy guards
'll shoot you
like a rabbit.

The country roads?

–Huh? He growls:
Early this morning on ours
I saw a moose track
higgledy-piggledy and full of blood,
and the season's ain't open yet!
Them poor animals, thinking they're still safe,
are hurrying for
town-posted land,
right past them Jones' boys.

–Jones boys?

Outlaws!
Live in that beat-up
place up the road.
Run a ring that
sells wild meat.
Hunt year round.
Likely shot
my wife Hazel's missing puppy.

Then I'd best rent a video in the village
and stay home!

Good idea, grumbles Ted,
swivelling back to his own.
But in case there's stray shots,
sit clear of the window!

Grief

I lean from this moonlit bridge and look upstream
at the Tomifobia splashing through
an old mill-race,

when a perfect silvery sphere,
foam,
comes drifting.

It's maybe too much liquor,
but, I swear,
it could be a woman's face.

–A vision from grief's
often exquisite excess
so irresistible that

when she slips
from sight under the coping,
I rush across the arch to keep her in view.

O where have you gone
Romantic, chromotint Indian maid
self-flung from a shoreside Lover's Leap?

Or pale, long-tressed
frontier Susanna spilt
by the loss of her bosom friend?

There you are, re-emerging
to float still-faced, incandescent,
mutely moonwards.

(Though, only in dream-realms, do the irreparably lost
float face-up. The drowned and adrift here on Earth
stare at the darkened bottom.)

You're a ghost,
yet I cling to you,
gazing wet-eyed downstream,

unable to blink
as you grow tiny,
drop through glinting rapids.

Far Gone: Remembering Robert Allen, 1946-2006

Wrung by worry,
I hug my oldest, dearest buddy
–grey and fleshless–
and stumble back to my car.

Fleeing dreadful portents,
I set about chores:
try reaching
before it shuts
the nearest town's hardware
to price new storm windows, doors.

–Take the cut-off over broken country.

Rising into the hills, I find
fall's far gone.
The border range juts up
knife-edged, charcoal, ugly.

Down along the river, maples and birches
vermillion and gold last week
are a bare crooked fright.

Crossing the swamp on a dirt road,
mind on winter readiness,
I swerve to avoid fresh logging ruts
scraping from the bush,

skid out,
bog down on a beaver dam
–scramble from my car cursing.

In the middle of nowhere,
slump on a log,
grab my cell-phone.

Then realize we'll never
race across far hills
to rescue each other again.

To Hazel Walker

–d. 2003

A bush rambler even after dark,
I hike up the old rail berm to the narrows,
where the river sprints thick and glinting
over a black scoop of slate.
Under the moon, a water-fog uncurls,
spirals like ghosts of the old Abenaki gods,
throngs downstream,
in a thick rising plume,
to a silver-edged collector pool.

I always follow the caving bank there,
where sometimes a muskrat, this time a beaver,
startled, veers at the apex of a gilt-edged "v,"
before plunging, tail-whomps the water:
boom! In warning of either man or beast....
"I don't walk there alone at night,"
you once warned me. "There's wolves!"

Shuffling though sodden swale grass, I think:
Tonight, there's just me,
not the four-leggeds, since
despite your lively folk fears, Hazel,
the wild dogs always hide from men:
leave tracks seen in daylight flecking the berm,
are spotted as night glitter or sometimes,
at the day's red edges, from the bush line
eyeing you on your tractor. They're shy,
elusive, swift. I see traces everywhere
and yet have only ever spotted one.

Hazel, have you joined them?

Redneck Genesis

From the bush back of roller coaster roads
pastures spill gleaming and anonymous
like snaps from fumbled garage sale albums.
In a box-shaped clearing slumps a derelict trailer,
sag-backed by a kitchen tip from which protrudes
broken TV's, dirt bike bits, a gold toy
World Wrestling Federation Championship belt
in a final bout with rank gone-to-wild tulips.

IV. Meditations While Standing Among Cut Wheat

Meditations While Standing Among Cut Wheat

I

Teeth, generated by desire
grind down in the mouth's hollow
till we are nothing but worn out horse-laughs
interred in a bald pasture.

The plump and beautiful hooves
youth bears and is borne upon
chase nothing that lasts.
They are reduced to pits of leaking blood
or become pale horny curls
–the unshod feet of goats
penned all winter in a barn.

II

In a country of bent flame
loins scorch past all sufficing,
secrete their volatile napthas,
self-consume in fruitlessness.

For what is to be done
beyond a groan and a tight song
for us idiot claimants
clapped to our rocks,
addicted to the worm warren of our bowels?

Nothing. No thing.
In this cornfield, lovely at twilight,
I turn from the void,
from the crevices of words and cravings
to the smooth slippage of my own shadow.

Like some wild bindlestiff or sage,
it flows on the rows of smashed wheat,
the scattered grains of brief reprieve,
the contending fields of dark and light.

Written on My Fortieth Birthday

Up this big ridge I hurried
through birdsong
and a million stout young trees
that lean from the baby-blue lake below
like children with light on their backs
fleeing some great disaster.

High up now on the divide,
by a baldtop the wind thins,
I spot another lake to the west.
Darker than this first
it foots another sloping forest.

The light fails slightly.
I start off down
through bird-tunes
that drop with me
and pine stands that lean
as sharply as those others,
but which now seem like men
trying to draw up short
before a further great disaster.

Untitled I

Falling straight down, rain
makes tight rings in the river pool,
framed by wider, eddying spheres
where shore willows release vast drops....

May my poems be like these:
loaded by clouds into wild tops,
gathered and converged by countless
    twigs and leaves,
then released, full of the sky's
    grey-gold palette,
the taste off ancient trees.

Four A.M. Piece

From where
  are we talking about?

From the night's edge.

Let the half-light
    do the talking....
Listen to your
  dawn-mutterings, when
    the eye-sockets of language
      are shadows.

Here is your limberlost
  canoe-camp talk,
where the snipped, watch-spring stars
    hang-out,
and from opposite sides of the lake
  an owl and a loon
    make gothic chitchat....

What poetry loves is solitude,
  the wake of conscious prostration
      or disaster.
    It likes to trek and dabble
      in the Burn,
the lithe, deep-bottom voice,
      the dark fish rising
    lonely at sundown
        (or dawn)
at the mouth of a Lovelorn River.

Not just talk–
          utterance.

To write like this,
        get struck
    the only way that matters...
out of nowhere,
    out of a blind spot.
        Have the light
    at the tunnel's end turn
into the proverbial stormlamp
        wielding another train.
    Suffer an earthquake
        on your wedding day.

The only consolation is the language
        that'll catch you up,
string a taut wire through your gape,
    and drag you down
        to writhe and splutter
            in its wake.

It's the lingo that
    nightsides you,
        turns you black,
            wide-bodied,
with a pickerel's moony eyes–
    the better to observe how,
        under your shallow boat,
            gorgeous shadows
        have clustered all along.

Poetry

It visits mostly
when I go tramping
fields and woods.
It arrives as on a scented spring dawn
when after working late,
I paced the bushline
and heard the lovely sharp wrangling of fox pups
rough-housing in first territories;
or the time on a red evening,
after a day's drudgery
I crept quietly into tall rushes.
I had become transfixed repeatedly with how,
after my final intruding step
the stark fresh shout of peepers
snapped off perfectly
like green volcanic glass.
Their fresh chant gathered me in,
then poised me.
So poetry comes and goes with me, despite
I'm beside myself with worries.
There exists this world of fine, pure solitude,
perfect intimacy with strangeness
and seizing sounds and soundlessness.
Was this not how it was when the gods
visited men?
Now there are no gods–
just sheer wild intercessions
along a spruce-line, down a stream-crossed trail.

Crouching Tiger

(Written upon turning 60)

Late afternoon, roaming the bush lot:
What radiant almost visionary foliage!
Fall beauty I've read somewhere
only matched in China.

Leaves golden like the robes of the Emperor,
and crimson as the paper enfolding alms
good citizens as a matter of course
would furnish a beggar
since custom said he may one day be ruler!

–For legends told of Worthies
wrongly banished from the Court
to years of wandering
the "Lands of Lakes and Rivers,"
dwelling in the wilds as "Crouching Tigers"
till, vindicated,
they returned in glory to
mount the Dragon Throne.

What is it I seek in this glimmering,
thinning realm?
Great renown? Riches?
Restorative waters?
A remote clearing, where some lunatic
or forest buddha

beckons from his
chime-hung, glue-board temple?

Will the next trail-bend tell?

In a loggers' slash
edging a beaver pond,
blue jays flash,
twisting, maybe scoffing.

High up a lone yellow birch,
(spared to reseed the cut),
an old heron's nest sways:

A hobo's pack shucked
en route to the rising moon.

Postlude

For Robert Allen

Thus my days are past
In contradiction: with no skill to part
Vague longing, haply bred by want of power....
–William Wordsworth, "The Prelude."

Right you are, Bill! So let's cry on a green
shoulder. Suck a clover. Have a shot of mellow
Nature....

Last night late, a writer friend and I got back
from our annual fishing trip. We caught nothing–
among the sort of wet-footed crags
you'd like, Bill.
Over a beer, crest-fallen and empty-handed
we commenced discussion of our *angst*
(–a philosophical disorder, Bill: One of Mad George's
imports!).
We're all Romantic atheists now....
I, for instance, want religion
and the faith to believe.
Only thing is, if I had the faith to believe in the first place
then I wouldn't need the religion!
How's that
you old psychologist, for peeling
the onion a little deeper?

My friend nodded.
Then he turned the discussion to Nature.
(A good move those and these days, Bill, like raising
the subject of women. Though neither quite

constitute a religion!)
If, my friend declared, I loved the green muse
any more, I'd be William Wordsworth!
It's true–doubly–
though for all that I rarely catch my fish.
(They've strip-logged those Greenhead Ghylls, Bill.)
You'll find me sometimes sauntering
"voluptuously through fields and walks,"
crying up the merits of wasting time
like you did
–that is, you mildewed old hypocrite,
till the literary zeal and just plain ambition fired up
and fretted you back to your desk and London.
You two-timing, double-talking old coot,
I bet you spent more time
inditing about glades than rambling in them.
Me too!
I put my worries in writing and so answer them.
Also I bet you record
your present reward in heaven more
than enjoy it. There's the rub,
isn't it Bill? Whatever it's all about,
the only thing that really supplants the hunger
for God, Nature, Satori or even Satan
is the getting of the hunger down. It
irks us writers
does this beautiful world, green and godless.
It, (read Nature here...) ain't enough!
What's rougher is: *if it was,*
we wouldn't *need* it so much,

would we, Bill? Only the green
cragged need's enough–the vague longing,
the want of power–
which is the real catch-all infinitude
the poem watches getting us down....

Departures

There is a country I visit
    under starshine now
or in blue moonlight's
        terra incognita.

For me
    this is a departure.
I was a compiler of
        daylight fact:
my brain wasn't quiet
    till I had secured every ravine,
conquered every hill,
    and logged the correct term
        for each flower....

By head-rote I acquired
    what I should have gained
                by heart
    and thereby learned:
the sites and names of everything
    trespass against enchantment.

Despite such insight
    what's left recovers slowly.
Like a rare nocturnal animal
    it shies at the shadow.

Night discovers me again
    in this sidereal meadow.
The land tilts to a spruce swamp
            dreaming fog.
        Coyotes hunt here....

To my left, one croons
    and my mind lunges that way.
I recall the tale of a farmer
    waking one night
to the bangs of his husky
        gone off its chain.

The next spring,
    its lunar eyes flashed
blue dozens from the bushline.

V. Country Dark

Wolverine Propositions a Canadian Girl

I know you wish you didn't
want
another drink
especially at the expense
of one like me
hunched uncomfortably on this stool
in a swamplit tavern, birchbark shine of seltzer bottles,
my teeth too white,
my black hair shiny,
as Raven's wing,
my eyes blue balls of foxfire.

Peter Wolverine's the name:
won't you relax and savour
one other nightcap
distilled from glowing ladyfern damps,
vole blood, juice
of strangled swamp iris
to dye your dreams bluewhite
like the coat of a snow-weasel
waltzing among mice
on a blade
of winter light.

Fay

Things one loves most
rarely have the time for each other:
have you noticed?

Usher her,
the lovely Dolores of your wildest dreams,
to your secret, red-watered, salmonoid pool,

note unhappily how as you hymn the riffle,
her matchless eyes
perceptibly drift sideways,

then away,
(unless you proffer a gracious comparison)
though later when your *grande affaire's* passé

she'll remind you
(in the spirit of friendly solidarity)
about that wonderful, unforgettable

hiking and fishing trip.
She'll be unable to recall exactly
where the sublime brook rushed

nor has a moment right now
for you to refresh her recall,
though every time you still wander there,

her lovely absence haunts the spot
like a svelte wild trout,
twirling and glittering,

uncatchable,
in exile from her own memory,
still deep in yours,

witch of a lonesome watery-glade,
fey, rising to the soaked
long-tailed fly of your sadness.

Country Dark

Beyond my cabin walls
the bare, creaking woods....
Only night-murmurs now
from crickets freezing in funeral
suits of dew.

The next farm over
the mutt howls at length,
then stifles all
but his yipping
at a bad dream
or tumbling star.

I still myself too.

Cold, wild-eyed on this bed,
I think
of thinking no more of you.

Reading the Russians in a Country Restaurant

Abandoned like an old boot,
my poor heart's one big, cold ache
after last night's break with my lover.

When love's thwarted or lost, I turn to the Russians:
Chekhov, Akmadulina, Brodsky, etc.:
those somber and passionate restorationists of the heart.

On damp sheets they embroider a forlorn memory
of lovers pressed together for the last time, as for the first,
while, outside, aspens shiver off their gold.

Oh, if I'd their canon of heartbreak,
I could drown in grief memorably, allude captivatingly
to "The Canadian Lady with the Pet Dog"... beaver,
moose....

Yet, taking up my own pen, I am a dour,
mumbling muzhik whose tongue's memorials
run as coarse as homespun socks or handkerchiefs....

Hunched in the Ayer's Cliff Restaurant,
I sit here scribbling for all I am worth.
Lady, you left me and it hurts so bad.

Beyond the Outskirts

Squinting tearfully into the snow's glare,
I cut back through the meadows,
bearing my head like a giant egg
cracked by last night's session in a country bar.

No longer bar-queued with other males
expelled by their women
and listing in a Sargasso of loss, beer and juke-box shanties,
I am alone beyond the outskirts
on a trail devoid even of snowmobilers.

Sucking the quickening wind,
sniffing the cedars and snow melt.
I am heroically exercising and taking country air
–the only seltzer I know for heartbreak and a hangover.

Spring crows whirl above the sap-rise maples,
woodpeckers drum roll, and jays emend blue shadows.
In this vivid and releasing world
I puff and sweat beneath ridge tops
gone gold as improbable reconciliation.

Sleeping in the Country House Parlour

My woman's gone: so forget
sleeping lonely in the upstairs double!
I'll make my camp before the stove.
What a strange, shadowy, off-trail formation
and weird brush: stark garage-sale furnishings,
angular bric-a-brac lamp....
And now the lights off, me rolled in my bag,
what odd sounds from critters!
Howls from half-wolves next door,
crawl-space coon squeaks,
a porcupine gnawing at plywood glue,
like a slow buzz saw.
Closer yet, on the turntable,
the needle at the end of an old LP,
pounding, pounding
like a mad trapper at my cabin door.

Spring Relic

After Buson

On the farm porch melts
a last, grey cairn of snow.

What for him remains
after an endless winter
of besetting blizzards and
piercing lonesomeness?

Flung here by her last fall,
neither recovered nor replaced,
a corroded-purple key.

Surprises

Sometimes
the time is so long between

like an old mountain
a man forgets all.

He is surprised by an offer
but also more–that the terrain of
self, itself is found
changed,

a presumed green and
lushness lost,

the familiar forest scraped,
the heart reduced
to the moon's chilled pond.

It's the same with you I'm sure

which makes for one more shock:

the dealing of
parts of our selves
back and forth here
in this dark Algoma motel

pieces which glitter in the palm
as ruby-grained and beautiful
as petrified wood.

A New Relationship

I wield a shovel by my country house stoop
preparing a long neglected flower bed,
chopping at the knotty roots
of unpruned perennials, unburying
cast-off beer caps,
bent nails, screws....

She readies the new plants:
buttery yellow day lilies,
crimson columbine, pansies, lily-of-the-valley,
brought down that morning from her plot in the city.
She remarks: "It's important whether
a couple can garden together!"

And I shrug,
chuckle and assert:
"Most men are hunters, primarily.
It's probably different hardwiring..."
and play-toss the shovel
at the brush pile, javellin-like.

Still, I help her transplant
and feel sure that in her eyes I
have come up to snuff, and shown my stuff.
Then, in a final savvy touch,
I haul up rocks from the river
to neatly edge the bed.

VI. Return to the Tomifobia Valley

Spring Insight

A blackbird on a cattail
cocks his head and stares.

It is a pleasure to be
again in the vision of birds.

Loony Tune

Spring now and the moon's close up.
Oh warm-up comedian, cartoon character, all of us
  get the joke,
applaud and love your subtle silver engagement.
We all worship your bouncing silver ball and en masse
  sing along
doing Nature's fresh work in time to Nature's work song,
pulsing out the measures of uninhibitable procreation.

Rollicking opening chords: round the sprouting bulbs
  of wild leeks,
nightcrawlers at twilight glimpse gay silver light high
  at the end of their tunnels.
They put on tuxedos of best dark slime, set out on
  the undulant climb after moonness.
Nocturnals turn out of their soilsacks: porcupines
  shuffle up the trick stairs of woodpiles
to grab a peek from the peak, while their quills
twitch and blurr like showgirl plumes when moonlight
  shimmers into the dressing room.
And smelt, thronging in the estuaries of brooks, jostle
  off their cabin fever,
hallucinate on their bellies the smooth touch of buckshot
  gravel at the heads of feeder streams.
They flutter their fins and by the millions are away!
May they make it past the nets: millions gliding past
  winnowing frets:
For when spring is trial, you, moon, also offer consolation.
You assure the fish that whatever comes to pass, one cosmic
  egg is lodged safe in the riverbottom sky;

–you assure old January, cuckolded by his nightclub baby
May, that there exists a constant symbol of inconstancy
bringing comfort;
–you assure an aging beauty (who took insufficient note
of Pastor Herrick's sermon on the ephemerality of roses)
that, fueled by unconsumable wisdom, she might still
retain the better part of the fire;
–you footnote the quivering yellow fingernails of old
men, ten lunicles that say: Look here! Death has always
peeked out at you. He does no more today;
–you arrest the raw and brutal youth by directing him
to your skull at the top of the sky
and say, now seek your proper relation and level!
For new though venerable moon, yours is a shriveled
aspect.
Vita brevis, luna longa: I expect you got those varicose
veins and cellulite
from standing on your feet too long just as Whitman
surmised
–quickening and sobering all things alike: Great
Lake shore,
suburban dog stare, bumpershine of city councillor's
Lincoln Continental,
and, last but not least, the poet's trope, and the brain
of the poor poet yearning to go ashore on you,
knowing all along he never shall, but fully compensated,
for sometimes at least his language arrives, then goes off
again like a rocket
for bright gas clouds and the starscapes beyond:
the other stanzas of this loony sprinkle.

So love of mine, Momma Lune, it's spring and you're
ball queen!
Enough with poetry: let's boogie to supralunary
rhythm-and-blues
–telescope our legs in and out while you,
enjoying a glamorous three-quarter shadow profile,
spin your gold disk over and over again, moonrock.
Let's do the Funky Turkey, necks outstretched, heads up,
beaks open to drown in moonspray,
let's be loosed, singing in sprung rhythm, with the billion
smelt bullioning up streams,
let us ravel like worms, sprawled in dew, our six hearts
beating in perfect harmony, our opposite orifices
crooning hermaphroditic junetunes to ourselves,
let's scribble verses, each word shining like hub caps
of Buicks lined up in lover's lane,
let's animate: let's wax to the Sylvester the Cat above,
fleeing the big bloated bulldog of a cloud,
all of us now, let's congregate, significate, let's loony tune
–in a landscape pulsing like a Saturday night crowd
at the band shell,
we'll collide and pursue each other,
we'll howl, scramble madly, light the dynamite stowed
in our pants,
we'll belt out of the hollow log of our winter selves off the
proverbial cliff and plummet giggling straight up in
the air.
While birds grin and whistle Stravinski, we'll rave out
all this jazz....

Return to the Tomifobia Valley

Remembering Ian Tate

I remember between shedding valley walls
coiled a dawn fog-bank
wind had curled off the lake to the north

–a looming ash-coloured scroll
that shut the rising sun
out of the aspen bottoms

then abruptly let it through
in a golden shuddering last leaf-spangled flood,
–an effect you dearly loved,

pointing your chin then nudging me
with the welcome prompting
of Nature's valedictorian and venerable lover,

–no doubt as you would now
with the winter finally over
were you here on this same river trail,

passing spring run-off cleansed gravel
tufted with green swale grass
washed, swept forward like women's hair

and specked with blue violets and first butterflies:
one Mourning Cloak and many lighter sorts
drying their bright yellow wings in the sun.

This Life

This long, winding riverbank
whitening in early May moonlight,
rollicking with ice-out,
black spruce foldings of ravine slopes,
half-blocking the grinding of tractor
trailers on highway 55....
Strange if this is it, stranger by far
than salvation or personal immortality.
Me, at twilight, picking my way
across a pale, ice flow littered plain.

Odd indeed, if this be *all,*
luminously meaningless, protean,
evanescent, sited in a Cosmos
like some endlessly unfolding, exploding diagram,
a fay keep raised in the marches of a diminutive
    yellow sun,
fey matter that only to itself matters....

Strange, weird, even appalling!
(Fear the only deity, first and last.)
But lovely too: delicate, animated,
glimmering like new lightning bugs in June,
or like that fog's incandescent sock,
there, lifting off the river bend,
thronging down towards the highway bridge
with patched abutments where, last year,

they fished out an old farmer, self-drowned.
I hardly knew him or he me, though once when
he caught me crossing his lots, rambling for no reason,
talking to myself loudly, he just grinned.

Beauty, and at times a little companionship.
The moon sets, trail muck frosts,
truck noise drops. Time to turn back.
Under the sharp, plunging glitter, the swish of blood
in my head waltzes amid immense silence.

Looking Across at the Stoke Mountains, *Cantons de l'Est*

You can't have those far hills,
worn nubs as blue at summer twilight
as the lake of some infinite hyacinth.
They are unfit for your pocket,
will not break when you fall.
Nor is there any lake back up there
clear as the quill of a tumbled angel's feather.
The lake that is, moans darkly
out of the taps of rooming houses
in a great, too attainable city.
Old mountains, old foldings of nothing....
Nod to them, then move on
leafed for an instant in your own horizon's gold,
your head filled with sapphire nothing.

Illustration

Stab wounds of autumn sumac.
Blue teardrop cry of the robin
noting the season
from the moulting
teddybear gold of the tamarack.
Crested milkweed floss....

So autumn halts
briefly over the caption:
that which must fall
is most lovely.

Autumn Dress Code

On exquisite edge, leaves model
red hues of goodbye.
One behind the other, each parades off
over the ranges
of ravishing departure.

Spruce-bogs
glow
with the Gauloises' cellophane
of last flies.

Sleek skunks
nightclub to the headlight electric,
sashay under helpless hurtling
pickups.

Having slaughtered my way to my cabin,
I'm spooked before sleep
by the flamboyant submission of their bones.

I'd forgot how
frost embalms grassblades,
silvers twigs, makes
fine grave-goods of seed-crowns.

I'm a survivor at the funeral.
I'm a wallflower among
fey dancing dandies.
I couldn't feel more out of it
in this will to live–
a cheap hand-me-down suit.

Autumn Revelation

Unhobbled from these roadside trees
rose-edged leaves submit
to those in this world that seek
there's nothing
more than falling
than land change, air change, sea change:
ladders of detachment,
leaves from their falling falling–
beyond the East Gate in wilderness time,
torn Adam in exile
red faced and lorn
still dreaming of Eve's arm
as it coils towards the apple
lovely in declining light.

Fall Descriptive

All things
in the forest
ceremoniously glisten.

I've hiked to the mountain-slope lake
to view

gold embroidery points
shed from a Queen and her Ladies' fingers,
in their sympathy with her
(face a sudden cloud-halved sun)
as she's informed by a winded, nervous courier
that on some distant strand
her ever neglectful
Crusader King

has fallen into the hands of Mussulmen,
never to be seen again.

–Her exquisite
formal
gesture of public sorrow

in submission to the Cold

: shoreline tamaracks in a yellow ring

dropping needles into the water
one
by
glinting one.

Zag

From these snows
bare elms
needle
a red horizon

which cards up cirrus
so high
it might be sky-silk
combed off another planet.

A tiny world zigs
blue-cheeked and white-capped,
caped by a blizzard of stars.

My rapt eye waters,
my mouth makes mufflers of breath.
Under winter skies I am
a lone man weaving home.

Sleepless

Wind pries
the roof shingles,
dislodging
one by one
the hours.

Glittering
through a frost-hole
in the window,
the same
insomniac star.

Fur Trade

Had I, instead of wandering
the forested back lot this fall,
re-stuffed the cabin walls,
January's subzero drafts
wouldn't numb my thighs.

True. But at night, writing here in my chair,
I'd not know how
over that snow-banked ridge,
beside the beaver pond spillway,
now all but frozen shut,

wolves ring and feast on a buck,
then convene on the big cap-rock
that overlooks the valley and my white roof
to celebrate their full bellies and wild estate
with stern and lovely ululations....

In this frost-spiked room,
momentarily immune from the cold,
I envision and hear them.
Like the wild things wintering in my walls,
my dreams eat the insulation.

VII. What the Landscape Wants

Evening View from the County Dump

Though milfoil stuffed and starved, the distant lake
disarmingly glows.
Rooted in this trash slope,
a survivor pine inscribes a fine arabesque
against the puce sky.

Weird kitsch!
An ailing vision of occult Northern-ness
to crown a stack of them
like so many splintered
and tossed window frames.

–The curdled spittle
of generations of Limberlost-foolish,
sappy poets,
dispelled for more plausible
if still less than artless light.

For I, too, have sinned,
unscrolled the prettily painted blind
over views of clearcuts and tips.

Fabricated and trafficked in bogus beauties....

Still, though I plead guilty
and stand convicted of
coy romance and cloying misrepresentation,
how this sight thrills me.
Entranced by the queer lake light,
the branch-clambering star,
the blue phosphorescing dump,
I scavenge after the right words
like a starved coon in a heap of tins.

Curse on the Despoiler of the Hackett Stream

Let the young engineer
who thirty years ago
drew up the plans begetting the throughway
whose culvert bottles this

once-delightful brook,
barring and wiping out
its remnant tribe
of red and gold-flecked trout–

while enjoying retirement one day:
motor-homing grandly overhead
savouring at leisure
personal milestones,

nod off at the wheel,
swerve, roll, get flung out,
crawl scraped, sore, confused
up this slimy, step-sectioned, insurmountable tube.

Thoughts While Hiking

Up the trail, wind
parts the trees,
like a local boy
drawing a bead.

Did one of them hole
this No Hunting / Town-Limits sign?

Killer November.
The Season's in a week.
–Meaning for City Escapees
and the Meek:
fretting housebound,
or risking lead-poisoning.

I'll head towards town.

What's this?
Just off the trail,
moose prints
still flooding.

–Moving town-wards too:
To improve its odds?

Do they know these things?
Maybe.

But does it make a difference?

Do we all flee what we figure's
after us,

while an outlaw back of a bush
lays his cheek along a rifle breech?

After the Deluge

Reaching the bluff's shoulder, a high clearing–
I stop on glacial sand to urinate
(welcome pause after hiking up panting
and greedily drinking from every spate!)

then flop down to rest, packstraps loosed, to sip
the prospect from this ancient sky-high beach.
Under a net of loggers' swathe and rip
May-flowered mountains hunch, range off and reach

deep into Quebec. There's the north divide,
creeks sawing each flank's straddled wishbone
of rich valley timber each hungry side
tears at. Last noon at the nearby border tarn

two minutes east of the rumrunners' shack
(these winters they run booze by snowmobile)
I took an international trout, swaybacked
that baked up to a bitter-tasting meal.

He was lean and tough: from lonesomeness I'd say,
or Reagan's special rain had vinegared him.
He'd stayed lovely. I can't tell you the way
the rose and eggshell blue stippled his skin

despite scars. Damn. There's still so much to save....
Few memories of gorgeous sights outlast
lilac and mauve twilight on a logged range,
or a gnarled survivor trout. Life recoups fast!

Locals found fresh cougar scat up here.
Lakes clear in ten years if nothing's been lost.
It's true. On the piss-soaked bank back there
a spout of thirsty swallowtails dips and twists.

A Man and His Life Must Be Completely Forgotten

So flash upstream, a salmon
muscling toward a fathering extinction,
dash across shallows to hang resting
if only for a moment
in lit amber deeps.

If we don't know what we are here to do
it is not to hang around
with those that think with certainty they do.

Watch for the meat caters:
bears with empty bellies in their heads.
Avoid the rancid pools of beavers:
All those who stage-manage memorable endings.

Create,
then clear up telltale relics.
The Creation, like a bright new cloud of fish,
must be unattributable.

Doomed, finish yourself entirely,
that you do not have to end again.
The wise man loves his offspring best
by giving them the most room.

What the Landscape Wants

is us, yanked past
in our strange missions.

There we go
scoring a grid
to sear ourselves on.

There we were, unstill,
churning up a road of dust.

What do we see?
Nothing.
We feel
the popping of small birds' necks.

Still
the landscape loves us....

It lunges
after us longingly
like a dog after
a familiar pick-up truck.

Untitled II

I

On this wild
   northern beach,
jobfree at last,
   I stretch my sky-hued tent
         fishbelly tight
   and make off feeling poetic.

I'm intent on finally doing
   nothing in particular,
here where there are only
   marvelous particulars,
on this lake-isle
   splayed like a vast Lot
      mineralized
for ignoring the divine injunction:
   not to look back
upon God's erasure and cleansing
   in the form
      (this time)
of a Wisconsinian ice-sheet....

Circling this place,
   I respond to mink tracks
delicately incising spits;
   wind-aria through white pike-grins;
            clay text
of indecipherable water-sculpted script;

and a bright red shore creeper
edging speculatively out,
then slithering back
like the “Z” in zen,
over a scraped white void of beach....

II

I’ve despoiled
this most perfect world
and myself again–
fleeing from my constructions
just to repeat them.
I circled an island
as an untasked being,
then retraced my tracks
in mind and fact
in order to contrive a poem.

Falling,
I tighten and tie
the world to my pole and pegs.
One blue heaven
thrumbs
while another sags, so a man
left to his restless self and vexed,
can wall and roof his own bright freedom.

Before Heading Back to the City Job

Dawn gilds the brook,
limns a shore-hung spider thread.

Time to quit playing Nature-boy, bud,
and get back!
Stop marvelling how the light
glimmers up the silk
like my yellow sedan
mounting the river-bridge to Downtown.

Tracing its path, my glance
strays over water to a spar
where suddenly I spot,
stationed like an early-bird boss,
a great-horned owl.

Huge-eyed, it throws me
a jaundiced look,
hoots scornfully,

then, with the sound of
a department photocopier
turned on full tilt,
swishes off to further
supervisory offices.

Citycountry

Climbing back of the cabin
    up the stream's spate,
I am in strong reverie:
    warblers vamp ecstatically.

Crepuscular light
    from the busted storm
stuns me too.
    –I am a green apostle,
a wide-eyed eremite
    glittering with rain-globes
off the needles I float through.
    I chant to myself:
        I belong here.

Then the old panic returns:
    I've been enlightened in this locale before
        till I wigged out.
I voiced bush lyrics
    (woven of blue-jay feathers,
        porky quills, weasel bones)
in a velcro and video age
    –trying to unleash a fresh poetic rage
but growing swamp-loco and plain loopy
    –a moon-weeper,
        coyote dueter,
forlorn wanker at country drive-ins,
    crazed by loneliness.
Again the city reared above the bushline of fantasy,
        in its beautiful
                blue poisoning of twilight,

seductive
    as a remote raptor's screams.

I return to the metropolis
    mostly willingly....
I strive within high close walls
        like an ancient Chinese poet
    reinstated to his rightful place
        in the great bureaucracy.
I make flying visits to that other country,
                hover a moment
like a street-lamp over a beaver pond,
                return again
to linger regretfully downtown,
            a firefly on a corner.
I'm an outlander in two different
            sites of dreams.

Here at the trail's top, finally,
            my mind rests.
Among half-shorn ridges
            the lake below blues off,
        a dog-legged dance floor
    in a smoke-filled Montreal *brasserie.*
Frogs chime like a truck of beer empties.
My face in this slopeside pool's
            a small pale cloud
hiking through a glass skyscraper's heart.

The End of Our World

On this Earth, inherited for a song,
a finale, describing how we, humankind,
smeared, bleared, blighted our Big Mom,
till one sweltering, short-of-breath day,
she played the ruthless charlady with her kettle
and boiled us like a dooryard nest of ants,
or torched us like a windrow of usurpatory
lime-splattering starlings, then,
humming a charming, restorative ditty,
lightheartedly sashayed on.

Milby Swamp

Back on the road through the once familiar swamp,
I search for what comfort this late winter scene affords....
At my feet, joining one half of the slough to the other,
a small ice-choked flow cuts the trail, draining round
a bare aspen into the larger of the two reservoirs. With my
toe, I probe the ice-jam at the aspen's base. Seven years
ago, this tree was pint-sized. In my memory's wateriness,
it seems always to be curvetting gracefully, slim leaves
aglow as when, during that distant spring, I startled an
ochre swamp sparrow from its hotel in the first green
fork. (For a moment, my ankles felt winged....) Much
water has gone underneath the bridge since then–or, more
accurately, flowed out beneath nearby Route 147 into the
slurry poisoned Coaticook River. Old sayings, intoned in
old swamps, ring right: Everything slips away, relentlessly....
Then, suddenly, I wonder otherwise. Shoving through
a spruce windrow, I mount a small rise and am startled by
an unchanged scene of alders, willows, and softening pond-
ice, plus a pair of beavers' stick castles. Transformation and
continuity–both are true, like a river below its fork–one
incoming tributary clear, the other soiled–both splicing in
a torrent through me. Over the years I thought that love,
its loss, the death of mentors and friends, and the brusque
awakening to personal limitation, had conspired to dam
me and reduce me, to stymie my brave start and all my
sweet joyfulness at this world.... I had stood in freezing
water too long, blood clogging, to believe that the day my
feet seemed winged might return. Like this pond, I felt
halved, and my growth logged to make a fence through

which all wild, natural things crept and fled away. But now there's flowing water at my feet and I hear myself singing. Some hibernating bird awakes; wild things venture back. Deep in these wet hill-bottoms, a stubborn startledness remains. On this sinking road, where Man and Nature have wrestled bitterly, the pond-ice glows yellow-green, cedars dream of their next fresh shoots, and revenant beings (even beavers despite the locals sure they were trapped out), drowse, dream, and wake. There comes to me this insight and pang, beautiful and fleet as a native trout: it is here I have resided all along! For all my migrations after love and city-gain, I have lived in this beaver hutch, that weathered nest, and beside this loosening stream.

Born in Coventry, England, in 1946, Steve Luxton immigrated as a child to Toronto, Canada. He gained a BA in Political Science and Economics from The University of Toronto, and an MA in Creative Writing from Syracuse University where he studied under W. D. Snodgrass, Philip Booth and others. Returning to Canada, he began his teaching career, and has taught literature at Champlain, Vanier, and John Abbott Colleges as well as at Bishop's University in Lennoxville. In addition, he has taught creative writing for 25 years at Concordia University in Montreal. An original editor of both *Matrix* and *The Moosehead Review,* he has published four books of poems: *Late Romantics* (with Robert Allen and Mark Teicher), *the hills that pass by, Iridium,* and *Luna Moth and Other Poems.* His work has appeared in numerous anthologies, including *Anthology of 20th Century Poetry of the Eastern Townships, Co-incidences: Poètes anglophones du Québec, Cross/cut Contemporary English Quebec Poetry, Eternal Conversations: remembering Louis Dudek, The Lyric Paragraph, The Moosehead Anthology, The Other Language, Passions & Poisons, Poésie de Montréal Poems,* and *Quebec Suite.* He currently lives with his wife Angela Leuck in Montreal and near Ayer's Cliff in the rural Eastern Townships of Quebec.